Forever And Ever Amen

Forever And Ever Amen

A Time-Honored Way of Praying and Reading Scripture

Terry Rueff

Scripture quotations are taken from the
(NASB®) NewAmerican Standard Bible®,
Copyright © 2020 byTheLockman Foundation.
Used by permission. All rights reserved.
https://www.lockman.org/

Copyright © 2024 by Terry Rueff
All Rights Reserved

Cover Photograph by Terry Rueff
Copyright ©2024 by Terry Rueff
All Rights Reserved

Linda, thank you for your prayers and help with this project.
Your support gave me the confidence to write.
Love you.

Contents

Introduction	1
A Very Brief History	3
The Framework	7
Two Times A Day	11
Beginning Prayer	12
Later Prayer	15
Calendar Of Scripture Readings	19
November 27	20
January 27	24
March 27	28
May 27	32
July 27	36
September 27	40
November 26	43
Abbreviations	44
Bibliography	45
About The Author	46

Introduction

My wife Linda and I are blessed to have enjoyed hiking, bicycling, and paddling throughout the continental United States. The anticipation of seeing a new landscape is exciting. After climbing to the top of Yosemite Falls, which drops 2,425 feet to the valley floor, the view of Yosemite Valley is awe-inspiring. Biking the carriage roads in Acadia National Park gave us an intimate view of the forest, and we were amazed at the artistry expressed in the seventeen stone-faced bridges. Paddling in the Merritt Island Wildlife Refuge at night to watch the manatees swim and mullet jump, lit by the glow of bioluminescence, is unforgettable. But there is something to say for the familiar. A favorite hike of ours is in Carter Caves State Park in Kentucky. We know there is a fascinating arch and a waterfall at the beginning, several views of the lake, two short steep climbs after the swinging bridges, and, near the end, a choice of hiking above or below another arch.

Familiarity with the trail does not make it boring. It is comforting because we know the direction to head and roughly what lies before us. But nature is always in the process of change—sometimes subtle and sometimes dramatic. Wildflowers that bloom in April gradually give way to those that bloom in August. A trickling waterfall gushes after a summer thunderstorm. In fall, leaves change color and float to the ground. In winter, bare trees allow hidden landscapes to appear. The trail is the same—the experience is different.

For me, this is true in my daily prayer times that follow a set format with repeating Scriptures. I know the layout and some of the Scriptures I will read. However, the conversation with God and the meditations change depending on the joys and challenges I am experiencing. The insights given by the Spirit may be subtle or dramatic.

I have followed a path of structured prayer for more than 35 years, using different resources to guide me. However, no book, or set of books, included everything I wanted. They each had strengths I wish I could have included in *Forever And Ever Amen.* But everything has its trade-offs. I was looking for a thin, single-volume prayer guide that, in one year, I could read the books found in every Christian Bible. It needed limited choices in what to read on any given day. Finally, it had to echo a prayer format that began in the sixth century.

You may discover that *Forever And Ever Amen* does not contain the elements you want. Continue your search and find what will help draw you closer to God. If you follow this trail, I pray you will find it comforting and spiritually revealing.

Terry Rueff

One

A Very Brief History

> I remember the days of old;
> I meditate on all Your accomplishments;
> I reflect on the work of Your hands.
> I spread out my hands to You;
> My soul longs for You, like a weary land.
> —Psalm 143:5-6

Forever And Ever Amen is a variation of a prayer practice that goes back centuries. The author of Psalm 119:164 writes, "Seven times a day I praise You / Because of your righteous judgements." By the time Jesus walked this earth, there was a set hour for prayer. Acts 3:1 states, "Peter and John were going up to the temple at the ninth hour, the hour of prayer." Saint Benedict wrote his *Rule for Monasteries* during the sixth century. The instructions to his community of monks included set times to join together in prayer.

> Let us therefore bring our tribute of praise to our Creator 'for the judgments of His justice' at these times: the Morning Office, Prime, Terce, Sext, None, Vespers and Compline; and in the night let us arise to glorify Him

This grouping of times designated for prayer is known as the Divine Office. Benedict stipulated that these eight times include hymns, Psalms, other Biblical readings, and common prayers. Edward J. Quigley traces the history of the Divine Office in his book *The Divine Office: A Study of the Roman Breviary*, published in 1920. According to Quigley, Benedict's format underwent multiple revisions before being adopted by the Roman Catholic Church in 1145. The Reformed Breviary of 1568 is similar in structure to what was available in the 1920s. As of this writing, the latest revision, known as the *Liturgy of the Hours*, was in 1975.

In England, during the Protestant Reformation, Thomas Cranmer, the Archbishop of Canterbury, oversaw the formation of—and wrote much of—the Anglican *Book of Common Prayer,* first published in 1549. William Reed Huntington, the Rector of Grace Church New York, wrote a paper titled *A Short History of the Book of Common Prayer* published in 1893. Huntington states:

> Cranmer and his associates subjected the services of the hours to a process of combination and condensation. The office for the first three hours they compressed into An Order for Daily Morning Prayer ... and the Offices for the last two hours, namely, Vespers and Complene [sic], they made over into An Order for Daily Evening Prayer....
>
> These two formularies ... make the core and substance of our present daily offices.

The American Episcopal Church adopted the *Book of Common Prayer* in 1789. The Anglican Church of North America published the latest revision in 2019. Other prayer guides repeat this cycle of Psalms, standard prayers, and Old and New Testament readings.

All the books have different content to help guide you through a time of prayer. Some books include spiritual commentaries or traditional and modern hymns. Many follow a calendar with specific readings appropriate to a season, feast day, holy day, or saint. In most books, the texts for the repeated readings are printed. Scriptures read once a year are printed or referenced on a calendar. The result is a treasure trove of hymns, prayers, Scriptures, and writings. However, they require multi-volume works or a thick single book. The books may have sizable, but still limited, Old and New Testament readings. They may not be in a preferred translation. When read privately, decisions concerning what prayers to use are needed. Unfortunately, this can lead to distractions.

Forever And Ever Amen distills the collection of prayers into a few found in the Bible. It has a simplified Calendar Of Scripture Readings. Only the books found in all Christian Bibles are in the reading schedule. This allows more people to follow the readings and makes the quantity of Old Testament reading manageable. The Old Testament books will be read in one year, except Psalms, which is read ten times. The Gospels and the Book of Romans are read twice. The remainder of the New Testament is read once.

Two

The Framework

> I rise before dawn and cry for help;
> I wait for Your words.
> My eyes anticipate the night watches,
> So that I may meditate on Your word.
> —Psalm 119:147-148

The daily readings are divided between Beginning Prayer and Later Prayer. Beginning Prayer's purpose is to praise God, to read how He works throughout history, to pray for others, and to acknowledge the Father, Son, and Holy Spirit. It starts with a brief prayer and then Psalm 95 or four alternative Psalms. Next are additional readings from Psalms and the Old and New Testaments. On the Calendar Of Scripture Readings (found in the back of the book), the references to the readings are on the first line of the appropriate date. Following this is Luke 1:68–79, known as The Song (or Canticle) of Zechariah. He praises God's faithfulness and His plan for deliverance. Zechariah also rejoices in the part his son John the Baptist (and now we) will play in that plan. Next is a time to pray for others. Then Matthew 6:9–13, the Lord's Prayer, directs our thoughts toward, among other things, our sin and forgiveness. Next are Scriptures that remind the reader of some of the basics of the Christian faith. Finally, there is a prayer glorifying God.

Later Prayer is intended as a pause before bedtime to focus on God's help and Jesus' time on earth. It is also a time to thank God for what He has done today. Later Prayer starts with a prayer for help and a reminder of God's compassion. Then, one or more Psalms are read followed by a Gospel reading. On the calendar, they are on the second line of the appropriate date. Next, Luke 1:46–55, The Song (or Canticle) of Mary, is read. Hear Mary praise God for what "great things" (v. 49) He has done for her and His faithfulness. We should do the same. Next is the Lord's Prayer. The time ends with a prayer glorifying God.

Structure helps to focus and give direction to your prayer life. However, it is a framework that is adaptable to your needs. If you only have time to read the Old Testament in Beginning Prayer, read both New Testament Scriptures during Later Prayer. If you are short on time, walk through the written text and save the calendar Scriptures for later. If you want to read the Old Testament one year and Acts, the Epistles, and Revelation the following year, that is easy to arrange. I encourage you to include a daily Gospel reading to relive Jesus' birth, hear His teachings, see His compassion, watch His sacrificial death for us, or rejoice in His rising from the dead.

This guide promotes a time for giving thanks and praise. It also encourages a time of listening to and reflecting on the "living and active" word of God (Hebrews 4:12). I will make five suggestions to help that process. The first is to quiet your phone and watch so you can quiet your mind. Every beep, vibration, or ring will try to take priority over your meeting with the Father. The second is to leave your drink of choice on the counter. When it becomes too cold or warm to drink, it will take your mind off the sacred time you are experiencing. The time without those distractions may lead to the discipline of fasting. Who knows what that would teach you?

As explained earlier, prayers and Scriptures are read twice a day. The third suggestion is to choose the two times when your surroundings will be quiet. It may be different times on different days. If that is the case, you have to prioritize your time. Otherwise, events that seem more important than time spent with the

Almighty creep in. The fourth suggestion is to not catch up on missed readings during your time of worship unless you have extra time. That will become a distraction as you try to cram in everything. Spend time with the current day's readings and find another time to read the skipped Scriptures.

Finally, do not make this a Bible study. It is a time of prayer and reflection. Pulling out commentaries, concordances, or different translations will defeat the purpose. Don't get bogged down in names you can't pronounce, ancient medical treatments, and social practices that make no sense today. You can explore the complexity of historical details and nuanced meanings another time. Yes, this leads to a better understanding of Scripture, but it probably will not enhance your prayer, reflection, or listening in the moment. You are not in school studying. You are in a conversation with God.

Focus on the parts of Scripture that stand out to you. Let the Spirit show you new insights. See how God works throughout history, then examine your history. Praise God when the author is praising Him, repent when the texts point out sin, and thank God when the narrative reveals His blessing and faithfulness. As you read accounts of people struggling, share your struggles with Him. If the passage is giving instructions, ask for the strength to obey. Watch as Jesus walks through the dusty streets and pray for the faith to follow Him. Focus on the Scriptures before you while letting the Spirit lead you to a better understanding of your relationship with God.

Three

Two Times A Day

When we wish to suggest our wants to men of high station, we do not presume to do so except with humility and reverence. How much the more, then, are complete humility and pure devotion necessary in supplication of the Lord who is God of the universe! And let us be assured that it is not in saying a great deal that we shall be heard, but in purity of heart and in tears of compunction. Our prayer, therefore, ought to be short and pure, unless it happens to be prolonged by an inspiration of divine grace.

—Benedict

And when you are praying, do not use thoughtless repetition as the Gentiles do, for they think that they will be heard because of their many words.

—Matthew 6:7

Beginning Prayer

Psalm 51:15

> Lord, open my lips,
> So that my mouth may declare your praise.

Psalm 95 (For variety use Psalm 3, 24, 67, or 100)

> Come, let's sing for joy to the Lord,
> Let's shout joyfully to the rock of our salvation.
> Let's come before His presence with a song of thanksgiving,
> Let's shout joyfully to Him in songs with instruments.
> For the Lord is a great God
> And a great King above all gods,
> In whose hand are the depths of the earth,
> The peaks of the mountains are also His.
> The sea is His, for it was He who made it,
> And His hands formed the dry land.
> Come, let's worship and bow down,
> Let's kneel before the Lord our Maker.
> For He is our God,
> And we are the people of His pasture and the sheep
>   of His hand.
> Today, if you will hear His voice,
> Do not harden your hearts as at Meribah,
> As on the day of Massah in the wilderness,
> When your fathers put Me to the test,
> They tested Me, though they had seen My work.
> "For forty years I was disgusted with that generation,
> And said they are a people who err in their heart,
> And they do not know My ways.
> Therefore I swore in My anger,
> They certainly shall not enter My rest."

Psalm(s)

Readings

Luke 1:68-79 Song of Zechariah (The Benedictus)

> Blessed be the Lord God of Israel,
> For He has visited us and accomplished redemption
> > for His people,
> And has raised up a horn of salvation for us
> In the house of His servant David—
> Just as He spoke by the mouth of His holy prophets from
> > ancient times—
> Salvation from our enemies,
> And from the hand of all who hate us;
> To show mercy to our fathers,
> And to remember His holy covenant,
> The oath which He swore to our father Abraham,
> To grant us that we, being rescued from the hand of
> > our enemies,
> Would serve Him without fear,
> In holiness and righteousness before Him all our days.
> And you, child, also will be called the prophet of the
> > Most High;
> For you will go on before the Lord to prepare His ways;
> To give His people the knowledge of salvation
> By the forgiveness of their sins,
> Because of the tender mercy of our God,
> With which the Sunrise from on high will visit us,
> To shine on those who sit in darkness and the shadow of death,
> To guide our feet into the way of peace.

Prayer

> Pray for your family, friends, the needy, and the sick. Don't forget the farmer, store clerk, utility worker, and others who make it possible for you to have your needs and wants satisfied. Pray for the officials who serve in your city, state, country, and the world. Pray for the Church.

Matthew 6:9-13 The Lord's Prayer

> Our Father, who is in heaven,
> Hallowed be Your name.

Forever And Ever Amen

> Your kingdom come.
> Your will be done,
> On earth as it is in heaven.
> Give us this day our daily bread.
> And forgive us our debts, as we also have forgiven our debtors.
> And do not lead us into temptation, but deliver us from evil.

Reminders:

God the Father

> Do you not know? Have you not heard?
> The Everlasting God, the Lord, the Creator of the ends of the earth
> Does not become weary or tired.
> His understanding is unsearchable. (Isaiah 40:28)
>
> For God so loved the world, that He gave His only Son, so that everyone who believes in Him will not perish, but have eternal life. (John 3:16)

God the Son

> God, after He spoke long ago to the fathers in the prophets in many portions and in many ways, in these last days has spoken to us in His Son, whom He appointed heir of all things, through whom He also made the world. And He is the radiance of His glory and the exact representation of His nature, and upholds all things by the word of His power. (Hebrews 1:1-3)
>
> "Behold, the virgin will conceive and give birth to a Son, and they shall name Him Immanuel," which translated means, "God with us." And Joseph awoke from his sleep and did as the angel of the Lord commanded him, and took Mary as his wife, but kept her a virgin until she gave birth to a Son; and he named Him Jesus. (Matthew 1:23-25)
>
> For I handed down to you as of first importance what I also received, that Christ died for our sins according to the Scriptures, and that He was buried, and that He was raised on the third day according to the Scriptures, and that He appeared to Cephas [Peter], then to the twelve. (1 Corinthians 15:3-5)

> [B]ut He [Jesus], having offered one sacrifice for sins for all time, sat down at the right hand of God, waiting from that time onward until His enemies are made a footstool for His feet.
> Hebrews 10:12-3

> I solemnly exhort you in the presence of God and of Christ Jesus, who is to judge the living and the dead, and by His appearing and His kingdom: preach the word; be ready in season and out of season; correct, rebuke, and exhort, with great patience and instruction. (2 Timothy 4:1-2)

God the Holy Spirit

> I [Jesus] will ask the Father, and He will give you another Helper, so that He may be with you forever; the Helper is the Spirit of truth, whom the world cannot receive, because it does not see Him or know Him; but you know Him because He remains with you and will be in you. (John 14:16-17)

> Peter said to them, "Repent, and each of you be baptized in the name of Jesus Christ for the forgiveness of your sins; and you will receive the gift of the Holy Spirit. (Acts 2:38)

1 Tim 1:17

> Now to the King eternal, immortal, invisible, the only God, be honor and glory forever and ever. Amen.

Later Prayer

Psalm 70:1

> God, hurry to save me;
> Lord, hurry to help me!

Isaiah 57:15

> For this is what the high and exalted One
> Who lives forever, whose name is Holy, says:
> "I dwell in a high and holy place,

Forever And Ever Amen

> And also with the contrite and lowly of spirit
> In order to revive the spirit of the lowly
> And to revive the heart of the contrite."

Psalm(s)

Reading(s)

Luke 1:46-55 Song of Mary (The Magnificat)

> And Mary said: "My soul exalts the Lord,
> And my spirit has rejoiced in God my Savior.
> For He has had regard for the humble state of His bond-servant;
> For behold, from now on all generations will call me blessed.
> For the Mighty One has done great things for me;
> And holy is His name.
> And His mercy is to generation after generation
> Toward those who fear Him.
> He has done mighty deeds with His arm;
> He has scattered those who were proud in the thoughts of
> their hearts.
> He has brought down rulers from their thrones,
> And has exalted those who were humble.
> He has filled the hungry with good things,
> And sent the rich away empty-handed.
> He has given help to His servant Israel,
> In remembrance of His mercy,
> Just as He spoke to our fathers,
> To Abraham and his descendants forever."

Matthew 6:9-13 The Lord's Prayer

> Our Father, who is in heaven,
> Hallowed be Your name.
> Your kingdom come.
> Your will be done,
> On earth as it is in heaven.
> Give us this day our daily bread.

And forgive us our debts, as we also have forgiven our debtors. And do not lead us into temptation, but deliver us from evil.

Revelation 4:8

Holy, Holy, Holy is the Lord God, the Almighty, who was and who is and who is to come.

Four

Calendar Of Scripture Readings

As mentioned earlier, each date on The Calendar Of Scripture Readings (The Calendar) has two lines. The first line references the Scriptures intended for Beginning Prayer. The second line has the Scriptures for Later Prayer. For simplicity, The Calendar begins on November 27th, the earliest date for Advent in Western Christianity. The date of Easter changes every year, so the Lenten portion of The Calendar has to be adjusted by date.

Adjusting for Easter can be confusing at first. It involves taking the block of Lenten Scriptures—from Ash Wednesday to the Saturday after Easter—and moving them to the appropriate dates. Readings displaced by the Lenten Scriptures will be used starting the Sunday after Easter of that year. The Calendar has Easter on April 25th and Ash Wednesday on March 10th, their latest possible dates. To determine the date of Ash Wednesday, the start of Lent, find the date of Easter for the year in question. It will help to have a 2029 calendar in front of you as you read the following explanation. In 2029, Easter is on April 1st. To the right of April 1st, on The Calendar, you will see the number 24. Now go to Ash Wednesday on The Calendar—March 10th. Again, you will find a column of numbers to the right of March 10th. Move up The Calendar until you find the number 24. The date to the left of 24 is February 14th. That is the date for Ash Wednesday in 2029. (In a leap year, if February 29th falls within Lent, follow the standard instructions but subtract one from the final number.) You read the block of Scriptures from Ash Wednesday through the Saturday after Easter.

For the Sunday after Easter, return to February 14th, when you started reading Ash Wednesday's Scriptures in 2029. Begin reading the original Scriptures listed on that date, February 14th. These displaced Scriptures are read starting April 8th, the Sunday after Easter in 2029. Keep reading the displaced Scriptures in order until you reach May 2nd in any year. Starting May 2nd, you will be back on the regular schedule and will read the Scriptures indicated for the appropriate date. It is awkward, but it works.

The Calendar

Nov-27	Ps 1-4	Is 1-2	1 Tim 1:1–11
	Ps 5-6	Matt 24:1–35	
Nov-28	Ps 7-9	Is 3-5	1 Tim 1:12–20
	Ps 10	Matt 24:36–51	
Nov-29	Ps 11-15	Is 6-7	1 Tim 2
	Ps 16-17	Matt 25:1–13	
Nov-30	Ps 18	Is 8-9	1 Tim 3:1–13
	Ps 19-20	Matt 25:14–30	
Dec-01	Ps 21-22	Is 10-12	1 Tim 3:14–4:16
	Ps 23-24	Matt 25:31–46	
Dec-02	Ps 25-27	Is 13-14	1 Tim 5
	Ps 28-29	Matt 26:1–5	
Dec-03	Ps 30-32	Is 15-17	1 Tim 6:1–10
	Ps 33	Matt 26:6–13	
Dec-04	Ps 34-35	Is 18-21	1 Tim 6:11-21
	Ps 36	Matt 26:14–16	
Dec-05	Ps 37-38	Is 22-23	2 Tim 1:1–5
	Ps 39	Matt 26:17–30	
Dec-06	Ps 40-42	Is 24-26	2 Tim 1:6–18
	Ps 43-44	Matt 26:31–35	
Dec-07	Ps 45-47	Is 27-28	2 Tim 2:1–13
	Ps 48-49	Matt 26:36–46	
Dec-08	Ps 50-51	Is 29-30	2 Tim 2:14–26
	Ps 52-54	Matt 26:47–56	

Calendar Of Scripture Readings

Dec-09	Ps 55-57	Is 31-32	2 Tim 3
	Ps 58-59	Matt 26:57–68	
Dec-10	Ps 60-63	Is 33-35	2 Tim 4:1–8
	Ps 64-65	Matt 26:69–27:10	
Dec-11	Ps 66-67	Is 36-37	2 Tim 4:9–18
	Ps 68	Matt 27:11–26	
Dec-12	Ps 69-70	Is 38-39	2 Tim 4:19–22
	Ps 71	Matt 27:27–31	
Dec-13	Ps 72-73	Is 40-41	Titus 1:1–9
	Ps 74	Matt 27:32–44	
Dec-14	Ps 75-76	Is 42-43	Titus 1:10–16
	Ps 77	Matt 27:45–61	
Dec-15	Ps 78	Is 44	Titus 2
	Ps 79	Matt 27:62–28:10	
Dec-16	Ps 80-82	Is 45-47	Titus 3
	Ps 83	Matt 28:11–20	
Dec-17	Ps 84-86	Is 48-49	Gn 49:2-10
	Ps 87-88	Matt 1:1-17	
Dec-18	Ps 89	Is 50-51	Jer 23:5-8
	Ps 90	Matt 1-18-24	
Dec-19	Ps 91-93	Is 52-54	Judg 13:2-24
	Ps 94-95	Luke 1:1-25	
Dec-20	Ps 96-98	Is 55-57	Is 7:10-14
	Ps 99-101	Luke 1:26-38	
Dec-21	Ps 102-103	Is 58-59	Zeph 3:14-17
	Ps 104	Luke 1:39-45	
Dec-22	Ps 105	Is 60-62	1 Sam 2:1-8
	Ps 106	Luke 1:46-56	
Dec-23	Ps 107	Is 63-64	Mal 3:1-4
	Ps 108	Luke 1:57-66	
Dec-24	Ps 109-110	Is 65-66	Is 52:9-12
	Ps 111-113	Luke 1:67–80,	

Forever And Ever Amen

Dec-25	Ps 114-116	Is 9:1-6	Phil 2:5-11
	Ps 117-118	Luke 2:1-20	
Dec-26	Ps 119:1-40	Gen 1-2	Col 1:13-20
	Ps 119:41-88	Matt 2:1-12	
Dec-27	Ps 119:89-136	Gen 3-5	1 John 1
	Ps 119:137-176	John 1:1-18	
Dec-28	Ps 120-125	Gen 6-8	1 John 2
	Ps 126-129	Luke 2:21-52	
Dec-29	Ps 130-134	Gen 9-11	1 John 3
	Ps 135	Luke 3	
Dec-30	Ps 136-137	Gen 12-14	1 John 4
	Ps 138-139	Luke 4:1–30	
Dec-31	Ps 140-143	Gen 15-17	1 John 5
	Ps 144-145	Luke 4:31–5:11	
Jan-01	Ps 146-147	Gen 18-19	Heb 1:1–4
	Ps 148-150	Luke 5:12–32	
Jan-02	Ps 1-4	Gen 20-21	Heb 1:5–14
	Ps 5-6	Luke 5:33–6:26	
Jan-03	Ps 7-9	Gen 22-23	Heb 2:1–4
	Ps 10	Luke 6:27–49	
Jan-04	Ps 11-15	Gen 24	Heb 2:5–18
	Ps 16-17	Luke 7:1–35	
Jan-05	Ps 18	Gen 25-26	Heb 3:1–6
	Ps 19-20	Luke 7:36–8:15	
Jan-06	Ps 21-22	Gen 27-28	Heb 3:7–19
	Ps 23-24	Luke 8:16–39	
Jan-07	Ps 25-27	Gen 29-30	Heb 4
	Ps 28-29	Luke 8:40–9:9	
Jan-08	Ps 30-32	Gen 31	Heb 5
	Ps 33	Luke 9:10–36	
Jan-09	Ps 34-35	Gen 32-34	Heb 6:1–12
	Ps 36	Luke 9:37–56	

Calendar Of Scripture Readings

Jan-10	Ps 37-38	Gen 35-36	Heb 6:13–20
	Ps 39	Luke 9:57–10:24	
Jan-11	Ps 40-42	Gen 37-38	Heb 7:1–10
	Ps 43-44	Luke 10:25–11:13	
Jan-12	Ps 45-47	Gen 39-40	Heb 7:11–28
	Ps 48-49	Luke 11:14–36	
Jan-13	Ps 50-51	Gen 41	Heb 8
	Ps 52-54	Luke 11:37–12:12	
Jan-14	Ps 55-57	Gen 42-43	Heb 9:1–10
	Ps 58-59	Luke 12:13–48	
Jan-15	Ps 60-63	Gen 44-45	Heb 9:11–28
	Ps 64-65	Luke 12:49–13:9	
Jan-16	Ps 66-67	Gen 46-47	Heb 10:1–18
	Ps 68	Luke 13:10–35	
Jan-17	Ps 69-70	Gen 48-50	Heb 10:19–39
	Ps 71	Luke 14:1–24	
Jan-18	Ps 72-73	Ex 1-2	Heb 11:1–12:3
	Ps 74	Luke 14:25–15:10	
Jan-19	Ps 75-76	Ex 3-4	Heb 12:4–13
	Ps 77	Luke 15:11–16:15	
Jan-20	Ps 78	Ex 5-6	Heb 12:14–17
	Ps 79	Luke 16:16–17:10	
Jan-21	Ps 80-82	Ex 7-8	Heb 12:18–29
	Ps 83	Luke 17:11–37	
Jan-22	Ps 84-86	Ex 9-10	Heb 13:1–19
	Ps 87-88	Luke 18:1–30	
Jan-23	Ps 89	Ex 11-12	Heb 13:20–25
	Ps 90	Luke 18:31–19:10	
Jan-24	Ps 91-93	Ex 13-14	James 1:1–18
	Ps 94-95	Luke 19:11–44	
Jan-25	Ps 96-98	Ex 15-16	James 1:19–27
	Ps 99-101	Luke 19:45–20:19	

Forever And Ever Amen

Jan-26		Ps 102-103	Ex 17-18	James 2:1–13
		Ps 104	Luke 20:20–44	
Jan-27		Ps 105	Ex 19-20	James 2:14–26
		Ps 106	Luke 20:45–21:38	
Jan-28		Ps 107	Ex 21-22	James 3:1–12
		Ps 108	Luke 22:1–38	
Jan-29		Ps 109-110	Ex 23-25	James 3:13–18
		Ps 111-113	Luke 22:39–46	
Jan-30		Ps 114-116	Ex 26-27	James 4:1–12
		Ps 117-118	Luke 22:47–65	
Jan-31		Ps 119:1-40	Ex 28	James 4:13–17
		Ps 119:41-88	Luke 22:66–23:25	
Feb-01		Ps 119:89-136	Ex 29-30	James 5:1–6
		Ps 119:137-176	Luke 23:26–56	
Feb-02		Ps 120-125	Ex 31-32	James 5:7–12
		Ps 126-129	Luke 24:1–35	
Feb-03		Ps 130-134	Ex 33-34	James 5:13–20
		Ps 135	Luke 24:36–53	

Check for the start of Lent.

Feb-04	34	Ps 136-137	Ex 35	2 John 1
		Ps 138-139	Mark 1:1–20	
Feb-05	33	Ps 140-143	Ex 36-37	3 John 1
		Ps 144-145	Mark 1:21–39	
Feb-06	32	Ps 146-147	Ex 38-39	Jude 1:1–13
		Ps 148-150	Mark 1:40–2:17	
Feb-07	31	Ps 1-4	Ex 40, Lev 1-2	Jude 1:14–25
		Ps 5-6	Mark 2:18–3:6	
Feb-08	30	Ps 7-9	Lev 3-4	Rom 1:1–17
		Ps 10	Mark 3:7–35	
Feb-09	29	Ps 11-15	Lev 5-6	Rom 1:18–32
		Ps 16-17	Mark 4:1–20	

Calendar Of Scripture Readings

Feb-10	28	Ps 18	Lev 7-8	Rom 2:1–16
		Ps 19-20	Mark 4:21–34	
Feb-11	27	Ps 21-22	Lev 9-10	Rom 2:17–29
		Ps 23-24	Mark 4:35–5:20	
Feb-12	26	Ps 25-27	Lev 11-12	Rom 3:1–8
		Ps 28-29	Mark 5:21–43	
Feb-13	25	Ps 30-32	Lev 13	Rom 3:9–20
		Ps 33	Mark 6:1–13	
Feb-14	24	Ps 34-35	Lev 14	Rom 3:21–31
		Ps 36	Mark 6:14–29	
Feb-15	23	Ps 37-38	Lev 15	Rom 4
		Ps 39	Mark 6:30–56	
Feb-16	22	Ps 40-42	Lev 16-18	Rom 5:1–11
		Ps 43-44	Mark 7:1–23	
Feb-17	21	Ps 45-47	Lev 19-20	Rom 5:12–21
		Ps 48-49	Mark 7:24–30	
Feb-18	20	Ps 50-51	Lev 21-22	Rom 6:1–14
		Ps 52-54	Mark 7:31–8:13	
Feb-19	19	Ps 55-57	Lev 23	Rom 6:15–23
		Ps 58-59	Mark 8:14–38	
Feb-20	18	Ps 60-63	Lev 24-25	Rom 7
		Ps 64-65	Mark 9:1–29	
Feb-21	17	Ps 66-67	Lev 26-27	Rom 8:1–17
		Ps 68	Mark 9:30–37	
Feb-22	16	Ps 69-70	Num 1	Rom 8:18–30
		Ps 71	Mark 9:38–10:12	
Feb-23	15	Ps 72-73	Num 2	Rom 8:31–39
		Ps 74	Mark 10:13–31	
Feb-24	14	Ps 75-76	Num 3-4	Rom 9:1–5
		Ps 77	Mark 10:32–45	
Feb-25	13	Ps 78	Num 5	Rom 9:6–29
		Ps 79	Mark 10:46–11:26	

Forever And Ever Amen

Date	#	Psalms	OT / Gospel	Epistle
Feb-26	12	Ps 80-82	Num 6-7	Rom 9:30-10:21
		Ps 83	Mark 11:27–33	
Feb-27	11	Ps 84-86	Num 8	Rom 11:1–10
		Ps 87-88	Mark 12:1–27	
Feb-28	10	Ps 89	Num 9-10	Rom 11:11–24
		Ps 90	Mark 12:28–40	
Feb 29	If this falls within Lent, follow the instructions but subtract one from the final number. Choose any previous day for readings.			
Mar-01	9	Ps 91-93	Num 11-12	Rom 11:25–32
		Ps 94-95	Mark 12:41–13:31	
Mar-02	8	Ps 96-98	Num 13-14	Rom 11:33–36
		Ps 99-101	Mark 13:32–37	
Mar-03	7	Ps 102-103	Num 15	Rom 12:1–2
		Ps 104	Mark 14:1–26	
Mar-04	6	Ps 105	Num 16-17	Rom 12:3–21
		Ps 106	Mark 14:27–42	
Mar-05	5	Ps 107	Num 18-19	Rom 13:1–7
		Ps 108	Mark 14:43–65	
Mar-06	4	Ps 109-110	Num 20-21	Rom 13:8–15:13
		Ps 111-113	Mark 14:66–15:15	
Mar-07	3	Ps 114-116	Num 22	Rom 15:14–22
		Ps 117-118	Mark 15:16–32	
Mar-08	2	Ps 119:1-40	Num 23-25	Rom 15:23–33
		Ps 119:41-88	Mark 15:33–47	
Mar-09	1	Ps 119:89-136	Num 26	Rom 16
		Ps 119:137-176	Mark 16	
Ash Wednesday				
Mar-10	0	Ps 50	Joel 2:12-18 and Eccl 3:20	2 Cor 5:20-6:10
		Ps 51	Matt 6:1-18	
Mar-11		Ps 120-125	Num 27-28	Philem 1:1–7
		Ps 126-129	John 1:1–28	

Calendar Of Scripture Readings

Mar-12		Ps 130-134	Num 29-30	Philem 1:8–25
		Ps 135	John 1:29–42	
Mar-13		Ps 136-137	Num 31-32	1 Pet 1:1–12
		Ps 138-139	John 1:43–2:12	

1st Sunday of Lent

Mar-14		Ps 140-143	Num 33-34	1 Pet 1:13–2:3
		Ps 144-145	John 2:13–3:21	
Mar-15		Ps 146-147	Num 35-36	1 Pet 2:4–10
		Ps 148-150	John 3:22–36	
Mar-16		Ps 1-4	Deut 1	1 Pet 2:11–3:7
		Ps 5-6	John 4:1–26	
Mar-17		Ps 7-9	Deut 2-3	1 Pet 3:8–22
		Ps 10	John 4:27–38	
Mar-18		Ps 11-15	Deut 4	1 Pet 4:1–11
		Ps 16-17	John 4:39–54	
Mar-19		Ps 18	Deut 5-6	1 Pet 4:12–19
		Ps 19-20	John 5:1–15	
Mar-20		Ps 21-22	Deut 7-8	1 Pet 5
		Ps 23-24	John 5:16–30	

2nd Sunday of Lent

Mar-21		Ps 25-27	Deut 9-10	Rev 1:1–8
		Ps 28-29	John 5:31–6:15	
Mar-22	34	Ps 30-32	Deut 11-12	Rev 1:9–20
		Ps 33	John 6:16–24	
Mar-23	33	Ps 34-35	Deut 13-14	Rev 2:1–7
		Ps 36	John 6:25–59	
Mar-24	32	Ps 37-38	Deut 15-17	Rev 2:8–17
		Ps 39	John 6:60–71	
Mar-25	31	Ps 40-42	Deut 18-19	Rev 2:18–29
		Ps 43-44	John 7:1–13	

Forever And Ever Amen

Mar-26	30	Ps 45-47	Deut 20-21	Rev 3:1–13
		Ps 48-49	John 7:14–44	
Mar-27	29	Ps 50-51	Deut 22-23	Rev 3:14–22
		Ps 52-54	John 7:45–53	

3rd Sunday of Lent

Mar-28	28	Ps 55-57	Deut 24-26	Rev 4
		Ps 58-59	John 8:1–20	
Mar-29	27	Ps 60-63	Deut 27	Rev 5
		Ps 64-65	John 8:21–47	
Mar-30	26	Ps 66-67	Deut 28	Rev 6
		Ps 68	John 8:48–59	
Mar-31	25	Ps 69-70	Deut 29-30	Rev 7:1–17
		Ps 71	John 9:1–34	
Apr-01	24	Ps 72-73	Deut 31-32	Rev 8–9
		Ps 74	John 9:35–41	
Apr-02	23	Ps 75-76	Deut 33-34	Rev 10
		Ps 77	John 10:1–21	
Apr-03	22	Ps 78	Josh 1-3	Rev 11:1–14
		Ps 79	John 10:22–42	

4th Sunday of Lent

Apr-04	21	Ps 80-82	Josh 4-5	Rev 11:15–19
		Ps 83	John 11:1–16	
Apr-05	20	Ps 84-86	Josh 6-7	Rev 12
		Ps 87-88	John 11:17–37	
Apr-06	19	Ps 89	Josh 8-9	Rev 13:1–10
		Ps 90	John 11:38–57	
Apr-07	18	Ps 91-93	Josh 10	Rev 13:11–18
		Ps 94-95	John 12:1–11	
Apr-08	17	Ps 96-98	Josh 11-13	Rev 14:1–5
		Ps 99-101	John 12:12–36	
Apr-09	16	Ps 102-103	Josh 14-15	Rev 14:6–13
		Ps 104	John 12:37–50	

Calendar Of Scripture Readings

Apr-10	15	Ps 105	Josh 16-17	Rev 14:14-20
		Ps 106	John 13:1-30	

5th Sunday of Lent

Apr-11	14	Ps 107	Josh 18-20	Rev 15
		Ps 108	John 13:31–14:4	
Apr-12	13	Ps 109-110	Josh 21	Rev 16
		Ps 111-113	John 14:5–31	
Apr-13	12	Ps 114-116	Josh 22-24	Rev 17
		Ps 117-118	John 15:1–17	
Apr-14	11	Ps 119:1-40	Judg 1	Rev 18:1–8
		Ps 119:41-88	John 15:18–16:15	
Apr-15	10	Ps 119:89-136	Judg 2-3	Rev 18:9–20
		Ps 119:137-176	John 16:16–33	
Apr-16	9	Ps 120-125	Judg 4-5	Rev 18:21–19:10
		Ps 126-129	John 17:1–12	
Apr-17	8	Ps 130-134	Judg 6	Rev 19:11–21
		Ps 135	John 17:13–26	

Palm Sunday

Apr-18	7	Ps 136-137	Judg 7-8	Rev 20:1–10
		Ps 138-139	Luke 19:28-44	
Apr-19	6	Ps 140-143	Judg 9	Rev 20:11–21:8
		Ps 144-145	Luke 19:45-20:8	
Apr-20	5	Ps 146-147	Judg 10-11	Rev 21:9–27
		Ps 148-150	Luke 20:9-18	
Apr-21	4	Ps 1-4	Judg 12-13	Rev 22:1–21
		Ps 5-6	Luke 20:27-40	

Holy Thursday

Apr-22	3	Ps 89	Matt 26:14-29	John 13:2-20
		Ps 143	Mark 14:26-42	

Good Friday

Apr-23	2	Ps 31	Is 52:13-53:12	Heb 4:14-5:9
		Ps 51	John 18-19	

Holy Saturday

| Apr-24 | 1 | Ps 104 | Gen 2:4-3:24 and Gen17:1-10 | Ezek 36:18-37:14 |
| | | Ps 16 | Ex 12:1-13 | |

Easter

| Apr-25 | 0 | Ps 42 | Is 55:1-56:1 | John 20:1-23 |
| | | Ps 19 | Rom 6:3-14 | |

Monday after Easter

| Apr-26 | | Ps 7-9 | Judg 14-15 | Acts 1 |
| | | Ps 10 | John 20:24-21:11 | |

Tuesday after Easter

| Apr-27 | | Ps 11-15 | Judg 16-18 | Acts 2:1–13 |
| | | Ps 16-17 | John 21:12-25 | |

Wednesday after Easter

| Apr-28 | | Ps 18 | Judg 19 | Acts 2:14–41 |
| | | Ps 19-20 | Matt 28:1-20 | |

Thursday after Easter

| Apr-29 | | Ps 21-22 | Judg 20-21 | Acts 2:42–47 |
| | | Ps 23-24 | Mark 16:1-20 | |

Friday after Easter

| Apr-30 | | Ps 25-27 | Ruth 1-2 | Acts 3:1–10 |
| | | Ps 28-29 | Luke 24:1-24 | |

Saturday after Easter

| May-01 | | Ps 30-32 | Ruth 3-4 | Acts 3:11–26 |
| | | Ps 33 | Luke 24:25-53 | |

Begin reading scriptures displaced from Ash Wednesday until May 2nd.

May-02		Ps 34-35	1 Sam 1-2	Acts 4:1–22
		Ps 36	Matt 1	
May-03		Ps 37-38	1 Sam 3-5	Acts 4:23–31
		Ps 39	Matt 2:1–3:12	

Calendar Of Scripture Readings

May-04	Ps 40-42	1 Sam 6-7	Acts 4:32–37
	Ps 43-44	Matt 3:13–4:11	
May-05	Ps 45-47	1 Sam 8-9	Acts 5:1–11
	Ps 48-49	Matt 4:12–5:12	
May-06	Ps 50-51	1 Sam 10-12	Acts 5:12–16
	Ps 52-54	Matt 5:13–37	
May-07	Ps 55-57	1 Sam 13	Acts 5:17–42
	Ps 58-59	Matt 5:38–6:15	
May-08	Ps 60-63	1 Sam 14-15	Acts 6:1–7
	Ps 64-65	Matt 6:16–7:6	
May-09	Ps 66-67	1 Sam 16	Acts 6:8-7:40
	Ps 68	Matt 7:7–29	
May-10	Ps 69-70	1 Sam 17-18	Acts 7:41–53
	Ps 71	Matt 8:1–22	
May-11	Ps 72-73	1 Sam 19	Acts 7:54–60
	Ps 74	Matt 8:23–9:13	
May-12	Ps 75-76	1 Sam 20-22	Acts 8:1–3
	Ps 77	Matt 9:14–38	
May-13	Ps 78	1 Sam 23-24	Acts 8:4–8
	Ps 79	Matt 10	
May-14	Ps 80-82	1 Sam 25	Acts 8:9–25
	Ps 83	Matt 11:1–19	
May-15	Ps 84-86	1 Sam 26-27	Acts 8:26–40
	Ps 87-88	Matt 11:20–12:14	
May-16	Ps 89	1 Sam 28-30	Acts 9:1–19
	Ps 90	Matt 12:15–37	
May-17	Ps 91-93	1 Sam 31, 2 Sam 1	Acts 9:19–31
	Ps 94-95	Matt 12:38–13:23	
May-18	Ps 96-98	2 Sam 2-3	Acts 9:32–43
	Ps 99-101	Matt 13:24–30	
May-19	Ps 102-103	2 Sam 4-6	Acts 10:1–8
	Ps 104	Matt 13:31–52	

Forever And Ever Amen

May-20	Ps 105	2 Sam 7-8	Acts 10:9–23
	Ps 106	Matt 13:53–14:21	
May-21	Ps 107	2 Sam 9-11	Acts 10:24–48
	Ps 108	Matt 14:22–15:20	
May-22	Ps 109-110	2 Sam 12	Acts 11:1–18
	Ps 111-113	Matt 15:21–39	
May-23	Ps 114-116	2 Sam 13-14	Acts 11:19–30
	Ps 117-118	Matt 16:1–20	
May-24	Ps 119:1-40	2 Sam 15	Acts 12:1–19
	Ps 119:41-88	Matt 16:21–17:21	
May-25	Ps 119:89-136	2 Sam 16-17	Acts 12:19–25
	Ps 119:137-176	Matt 17:22–18:14	
May-26	Ps 120-125	2 Sam 18	Acts 13:1–3
	Ps 126-129	Matt 18:15–19:12	
May-27	Ps 130-134	2 Sam 19-20	Acts 13:4–12
	Ps 135	Matt 19:13–30	
May-28	Ps 136-137	2 Sam 21-22	Acts 13:13–52
	Ps 138-139	Matt 20:1–28	
May-29	Ps 140-143	2 Sam 23-24	Acts 14:1–7
	Ps 144-145	Matt 20:29–21:17	
May-30	Ps 146-147	1 Kgs 1	Acts 14:8–20
	Ps 148-150	Matt 21:18–46	
May-31	Ps 1-4	1 Kgs 2	Acts 14:21–28
	Ps 5-6	Matt 22:1–22	
Jun-01	Ps 7-9	1 Kgs 3-4	Acts 15:1–21
	Ps 10	Matt 22:23–46	
Jun-02	Ps 11-15	1 Kgs 5-6	Acts 15:22–35
	Ps 16-17	Matt 23	
Jun-03	Ps 18	1 Kgs 7	Acts 15:36–41
	Ps 19-20	Matt 24:1–35	
Jun-04	Ps 21-22	1 Kgs 8	Acts 16:1–5
	Ps 23-24	Matt 24:36–51	

Calendar Of Scripture Readings

Jun-05	Ps 25-27	1 Kgs 9	Acts 16:6–10
	Ps 28-29	Matt 25:1–13	
Jun-06	Ps 30-32	1 Kgs 10-11	Acts 16:11–15
	Ps 33	Matt 25:14–30	
Jun-07	Ps 34-35	1 Kgs 12	Acts 16:16–40
	Ps 36	Matt 25:31–26:13	
Jun-08	Ps 37-38	1 Kgs 13-14	Acts 17:1–9
	Ps 39	Matt 26:14–35	
Jun-09	Ps 40-42	1 Kgs 15	Acts 17:10–15
	Ps 43-44	Matt 26:36–68	
Jun-10	Ps 45-47	1 Kgs 16-17	Acts 17:16–34
	Ps 48-49	Matt 26:69–27:10	
Jun-11	Ps 50-51	1 Kgs 18-19	Acts 18:1–17
	Ps 52-54	Matt 27:11–44	
Jun-12	Ps 55-57	1 Kgs 20	Acts 18:18–28
	Ps 58-59	Matt 27:45–61	
Jun-13	Ps 60-63	1 Kgs 21	Acts 19:1–22
	Ps 64-65	Matt 27:62–28:20	
Jun-14	Ps 66-67	1 Kgs 22, 2 Kgs 1	Acts 19:23–41
	Ps 68	Mark 1:1–28	
Jun-15	Ps 69-70	2 Kgs 2-3	Acts 20:1–6
	Ps 71	Mark 1:29–2:12	
Jun-16	Ps 72-73	2 Kgs 4	Acts 20:7–12
	Ps 74	Mark 2:13–28	
Jun-17	Ps 75-76	2 Kgs 5-6	Acts 20:13–38
	Ps 77	Mark 3	
Jun-18	Ps 78	2 Kgs 7-8	Acts 21:1–16
	Ps 79	Mark 4:1–20	
Jun-19	Ps 80-82	2 Kgs 9	Acts 21:17–26
	Ps 83	Mark 4:21–41	
Jun-20	Ps 84-86	2 Kgs 10-11	Acts 21:27–36
	Ps 87-88	Mark 5	

Forever And Ever Amen

Jun-21	Ps 89	2 Kgs 12-13	Acts 21:37–22:21
	Ps 90	Mark 6:1–6	
Jun-22	Ps 91-93	2 Kgs 14-15	Acts 22:22–30
	Ps 94-95	Mark 6:6–29	
Jun-23	Ps 96-98	2 Kgs 16-17	Acts 23:1–11
	Ps 99-101	Mark 6:30–56	
Jun-24	Ps 102-103	2 Kgs 18	Acts 23:12–22
	Ps 104	Mark 7:1–23	
Jun-25	Ps 105	2 Kgs 19	Acts 23:23–35
	Ps 106	Mark 7:24–8:13	
Jun-26	Ps 107	2 Kgs 20-21	Acts 24
	Ps 108	Mark 8:14–38	
Jun-27	Ps 109-110	2 Kgs 22-23	Acts 25:1–12
	Ps 111-113	Mark 9:1–29	
Jun-28	Ps 114-116	2 Kgs 24-25	Acts 25:13–27
	Ps 117-118	Mark 9:30–50	
Jun-29	Ps 119:1-40	1 Chr 1-2:20	Acts 26
	Ps 119:41-88	Mark 10:1–31	
Jun-30	Ps 119:89-136	1 Chr 2:21-4:43	Acts 27:1–12
	Ps 119:137-176	Mark 10:32–45	
Jul-01	Ps 120-125	1 Chr 5-6	Acts 27:13–26
	Ps 126-129	Mark 10:46–11:26	
Jul-02	Ps 130-134	1 Chr 7-8	Acts 27:27–44
	Ps 135	Mark 11:27–12:12	
Jul-03	Ps 136-137	1 Chr 9-10	Acts 28:1–10
	Ps 138-139	Mark 12:13–37	
Jul-04	Ps 140-143	1 Chr 11-12	Acts 28:11–16
	Ps 144-145	Mark 12:38–13:31	
Jul-05	Ps 146-147	1 Chr 13-15	Acts 28:17–31
	Ps 148-150	Mark 13:32–14:11	
Jul-06	Ps 1-4	1 Chr 16-17	Rom 1:1–7
	Ps 5-6	Mark 14:12–31	

Calendar Of Scripture Readings

Jul-07	Ps 7-9	1 Chr 18-20	Rom 1:8–17
	Ps 10	Mark 14:32–65	
Jul-08	Ps 11-15	1 Chr 21-23	Rom 1:18–32
	Ps 16-17	Mark 14:66–15:15	
Jul-09	Ps 18	1 Chr 24-25	Rom 2:1–16
	Ps 19-20	Mark 15:16–32	
Jul-10	Ps 21-22	1 Chr 26-27	Rom 2:17–29
	Ps 23-24	Mark 15:33–16:20	
Jul-11	Ps 25-27	1 Chr 28-29	Rom 3:1–8
	Ps 28-29	Luke 1:1–25	
Jul-12	Ps 30-32	2 Chr 1-2	Rom 3:9–20
	Ps 33	Luke 1:26–45	
Jul-13	Ps 34-35	2 Chr 3-5	Rom 3:21–31
	Ps 36	Luke 1:46–66	
Jul-14	Ps 37-38	2 Chr 6	Rom 4
	Ps 39	Luke 1:67–2:21	
Jul-15	Ps 40-42	2 Chr 7-9	Rom 5:1–11
	Ps 43-44	Luke 2:22–40	
Jul-16	Ps 45-47	2 Chr 10-12	Rom 5:12–21
	Ps 48-49	Luke 2:41–3:20	
Jul-17	Ps 50-51	2 Chr 13-15	Rom 6:1–14
	Ps 52-54	Luke 3:21–38	
Jul-18	Ps 55-57	2 Chr 16-17	Rom 6:15–23
	Ps 58-59	Luke 4:1–30	
Jul-19	Ps 60-63	2 Chr 18-20	Rom 7:1–6
	Ps 64-65	Luke 4:31–44	
Jul-20	Ps 66-67	2 Chr 21-22	Rom 7:7–25
	Ps 68	Luke 5:1–26	
Jul-21	Ps 69-70	2 Chr 23-24	Rom 8:1–17
	Ps 71	Luke 5:27–6:11	
Jul-22	Ps 72-73	2 Chr 25-26	Rom 8:18–30
	Ps 74	Luke 6:12–36	

Forever And Ever Amen

Jul-23	Ps 75-76	2 Chr 27-28	Rom 8:31–39
	Ps 77	Luke 6:37–7:10	
Jul-24	Ps 78	2 Chr 29-30	Rom 9:1–5
	Ps 79	Luke 7:11–35	
Jul-25	Ps 80-82	2 Chr 31-32	Rom 9:6–29
	Ps 83	Luke 7:36–8:15	
Jul-26	Ps 84-86	2 Chr 33	Rom 9:30–10:21
	Ps 87-88	Luke 8:16–39	
Jul-27	Ps 89	2 Chr 34-36	Rom 11:1–10
	Ps 90	Luke 8:40–9:9	
Jul-28	Ps 91-93	Ezr 1-2	Rom 11:11–24
	Ps 94-95	Luke 9:10–36	
Jul-29	Ps 96-98	Ezr 3-4	Rom 11:25–32
	Ps 99-101	Luke 9:37–56	
Jul-30	Ps 102-103	Ezr 5-6	Rom 11:33–36
	Ps 104	Luke 9:57–10:24	
Jul-31	Ps 105	Ezr 7-8	Rom 12:1–2
	Ps 106	Luke 10:25–42	
Aug-01	Ps 107	Ezr 9-10	Rom 12:3–8
	Ps 108	Luke 11:1–28	
Aug-02	Ps 109-110	Neh 1-2	Rom 12:9–21
	Ps 111-113	Luke 11:29–54	
Aug-03	Ps 114-116	Neh 3-4	Rom 13:1–7
	Ps 117-118	Luke 12:1–21	
Aug-04	Ps 119:1-40	Neh 5-6	Rom 13:8–10
	Ps 119:41-88	Luke 12:22–48	
Aug-05	Ps 119:89-136	Neh 7-8	Rom 13:11–14
	Ps 119:137-176	Luke 12:49–13:9	
Aug-06	Ps 120-125	Neh 9-10	Rom 14:1–15:13
	Ps 126-129	Luke 13:10–35	
Aug-07	Ps 130-134	Neh 11-12	Rom 15:14–22
	Ps 135	Luke 14:1–24	

Calendar Of Scripture Readings

Aug-08	Ps 136-137	Neh 13	Rom 15:23–33
	Ps 138-139	Luke 14:25–15:32	
Aug-09	Ps 140-143	Est 1-3	Rom 16
	Ps 144-145	Luke 16:1–15	
Aug-10	Ps 146-147	Est 4-6	1 Cor 1:1–3
	Ps 148-150	Luke 16:16–17:10	
Aug-11	Ps 1-4	Est 7-10	1 Cor 1:4–9
	Ps 5-6	Luke 17:11–37	
Aug-12	Ps 7-9	Job 1-3	1 Cor 1:10–17
	Ps 10	Luke 18:1–14	
Aug-13	Ps 11-15	Job 4-6	1 Cor 1:18–2:5
	Ps 16-17	Luke 18:15–43	
Aug-14	Ps 18	Job 7-9	1 Cor 2:6–16
	Ps 19-20	Luke 19:1–27	
Aug-15	Ps 21-22	Job 10-14	1 Cor 3
	Ps 23-24	Luke 19:28–48	
Aug-16	Ps 25-27	Job 15-18	1 Cor 4:1–13
	Ps 28-29	Luke 20:1–26	
Aug-17	Ps 30-32	Job 19-21	1 Cor 4:14–21
	Ps 33	Luke 20:27–47	
Aug-18	Ps 34-35	Job 22-26	1 Cor 5
	Ps 36	Luke 21	
Aug-19	Ps 37-38	Job 27-29	1 Cor 6:1–11
	Ps 39	Luke 22:1–38	
Aug-20	Ps 40-42	Job 30-33	1 Cor 6:12–20
	Ps 43-44	Luke 22:39–46	
Aug-21	Ps 45-47	Job 34-36	1 Cor 7:1–16
	Ps 48-49	Luke 22:47–62	
Aug-22	Ps 50-51	Job 37-39	1 Cor 7:17–24
	Ps 52-54	Luke 22:63–23:25	
Aug-23	Ps 55-57	Job 40-42	1 Cor 7:25–40
	Ps 58-59	Luke 23:26–43	

Forever And Ever Amen

Aug-24	Ps 60-63	Prov 1-4	1 Cor 8
	Ps 64-65	Luke 23:44–24:12	
Aug-25	Ps 66-67	Prov 5-7	1 Cor 9:1–18
	Ps 68	Luke 24:13–35	
Aug-26	Ps 69-70	Prov 8-11	1 Cor 9:19–23
	Ps 71	Luke 24:36–53	
Aug-27	Ps 72-73	Prov 12-14	1 Cor 9:24–27
	Ps 74	John 1:1–34	
Aug-28	Ps 75-76	Prov 15-18	1 Cor 10:1–13
	Ps 77	John 1:35–2:12	
Aug-29	Ps 78	Prov 19-21	1 Cor 10:14–22
	Ps 79	John 2:13–3:21	
Aug-30	Ps 80-82	Prov 22-24	1 Cor 10:23–11:1
	Ps 83	John 3:22–36	
Aug-31	Ps 84-86	Prov 25-28	1 Cor 11:2–16
	Ps 87-88	John 4:1–26	
Sep-01	Ps 89	Prov 29-31	1 Cor 11:17–34
	Ps 90	John 4:27–54	
Sep-02	Ps 91-93	Eccl 1-2	1 Cor 12:1–11
	Ps 94-95	John 5:1–15	
Sep-03	Ps 96-98	Eccl 3-5	1 Cor 12:12–31
	Ps 99-101	John 5:16–47	
Sep-04	Ps 102-103	Eccl 6-9	1 Cor 13
	Ps 104	John 6:1–24	
Sep-05	Ps 105	Eccl 10-12	1 Cor 14:1–25
	Ps 106	John 6:25–59	
Sep-06	Ps 107	Song 1-5	1 Cor 14:26–40
	Ps 108	John 6:60–71	
Sep-07	Ps 109-110	Song 6-8	1 Cor 15:1–11
	Ps 111-113	John 7:1–24	
Sep-08	Ps 114-116	Jer 1-2	1 Cor 15:12–34
	Ps 117-118	John 7:25–53	

Calendar Of Scripture Readings

Sep-09	Ps 119:1-40	Jer 3-4	1 Cor 15:35–58
	Ps 119:41-88	John 8:1–20	
Sep-10	Ps 119:89-136	Jer 5	1 Cor 16:1–4
	Ps 119:137-176	John 8:21–47	
Sep-11	Ps 120-125	Jer 6-7	1 Cor 16:5–18
	Ps 126-129	John 8:48–9:12	
Sep-12	Ps 130-134	Jer 8-10	1 Cor 16:19–24
	Ps 135	John 9:13–34	
Sep-13	Ps 136-137	Jer 11-13	2 Cor 1:1–2
	Ps 138-139	John 9:35–10:21	
Sep-14	Ps 140-143	Jer 14-15	2 Cor 1:3–11
	Ps 144-145	John 10:22–42	
Sep-15	Ps 146-147	Jer 16-18	2 Cor 1:12–2:4
	Ps 148-150	John 11:1–37	
Sep-16	Ps 1-4	Jer 19-20	2 Cor 2:5–11
	Ps 5-6	John 11:38–57	
Sep-17	Ps 7-9	Jer 21-22	2 Cor 2:12–3:6
	Ps 10	John 12:1–19	
Sep-18	Ps 11-15	Jer 23-24	2 Cor 3:7–18
	Ps 16-17	John 12:20–50	
Sep-19	Ps 18	Jer 25-26	2 Cor 4
	Ps 19-20	John 13:1–17	
Sep-20	Ps 21-22	Jer 27-28	2 Cor 5:1–10
	Ps 23-24	John 13:18–14:4	
Sep-21	Ps 25-27	Jer 29-30	2 Cor 5:11–6:2
	Ps 28-29	John 14:5–31	
Sep-22	Ps 30-32	Jer 31	2 Cor 6:3–13
	Ps 33	John 15	
Sep-23	Ps 34-35	Jer 32-33	2 Cor 6:14–7:1
	Ps 36	John 16	
Sep-24	Ps 37-38	Jer 34-35	2 Cor 7:2–16
	Ps 39	John 17:1–19	

Forever And Ever Amen

Sep-25	Ps 40-42	Jer 36-37	2 Cor 8:1–15
	Ps 43-44	John 17:20–18:14	
Sep-26	Ps 45-47	Jer 38-39	2 Cor 8:16–9:5
	Ps 48-49	John 18:15–40	
Sep-27	Ps 50-51	Jer 40-41	2 Cor 9:6–15
	Ps 52-54	John 19:1–27	
Sep-28	Ps 55-57	Jer 42-43	2 Cor 10
	Ps 58-59	John 19:28–20:10	
Sep-29	Ps 60-63	Jer 44-46	2 Cor 11:1–15
	Ps 64-65	John 20:11–29	
Sep-30	Ps 66-67	Jer 47-48	2 Cor 11:16–33
	Ps 68	John 20:30–21:25	
Oct-01	Ps 69-70	Jer 49	2 Cor 12:1–10
	Ps 71	Matt 1:1–17	
Oct-02	Ps 72-73	Jer 50	2 Cor 12:11–21
	Ps 74	Matt 1:18–2:12	
Oct-03	Ps 75-76	Jer 51-52	2 Cor 13:1-10
	Ps 77	Matt 2:13–18	
Oct-04	Ps 78	Lam 1	2 Cor 13:11-14
	Ps 79	Matt 2:19–3:12	
Oct-05	Ps 80-82	Lam 2-3	Gal 1:1–5
	Ps 83	Matt 3:13–4:11	
Oct-06	Ps 84-86	Lam 4-5	Gal 1:6–24
	Ps 87-88	Matt 4:12–22	
Oct-07	Ps 89	Ezek 1-3	Gal 2:1–10
	Ps 90	Matt 4:23–5:12	
Oct-08	Ps 91-93	Ezek 4-6	Gal 2:11–21
	Ps 94-95	Matt 5:13–20	
Oct-09	Ps 96-98	Ezek 7-8	Gal 3:1–14
	Ps 99-101	Matt 5:21–37	
Oct-10	Ps 102-103	Ezek 9-11	Gal 3:15–22
	Ps 104	Matt 5:38–48	

Calendar Of Scripture Readings

Oct-11	Ps 105	Ezek 12-13	Gal 3:23–4:7
	Ps 106	Matt 6:1–15	
Oct-12	Ps 107	Ezek 14-15	Gal 4:8–20
	Ps 108	Matt 6:16–34	
Oct-13	Ps 109-110	Ezek 16	Gal 4:21–5:12
	Ps 111-113	Matt 7:1–12	
Oct-14	Ps 114-116	Ezek 17-18	Gal 5:13–26
	Ps 117-118	Matt 7:13–23	
Oct-15	Ps 119:1-40	Ezek 19-20	Gal 6:1–10
	Ps 119:41-88	Matt 7:24–8:13	
Oct-16	Ps 119:89-136	Ezek 21	Gal 6:11–18
	Ps 119:137-176	Matt 8:14–22	
Oct-17	Ps 120-125	Ezek 22-23	Eph 1:1–14
	Ps 126-129	Matt 8:23–34	
Oct-18	Ps 130-134	Ezek 24-25	Eph 1:15–23
	Ps 135	Matt 9:1–17	
Oct-19	Ps 136-137	Ezek 26-27	Eph 2
	Ps 138-139	Matt 9:18–34	
Oct-20	Ps 140-143	Ezek 28-29	Eph 3:1–13
	Ps 144-145	Matt 9:35–10:42	
Oct-21	Ps 146-147	Ezek 30-31	Eph 3:14–21
	Ps 148-150	Matt 11:1–19	
Oct-22	Ps 1-4	Ezek 32-33	Eph 4:1–16
	Ps 5-6	Matt 11:20–24	
Oct-23	Ps 7-9	Ezek 34	Eph 4:17–32
	Ps 10	Matt 11:25–30	
Oct-24	Ps 11-15	Ezek 35-36	Eph 5:1–20
	Ps 16-17	Matt 12:1–14	
Oct-25	Ps 18	Ezek 37-38	Eph 5:21–33
	Ps 19-20	Matt 12:15–21	
Oct-26	Ps 21-22	Ezek 39	Eph 6:1–9
	Ps 23-24	Matt 12:22–37	

Forever And Ever Amen

Oct-27	Ps 25-27	Ezek 40-41	Eph 6:10–20
	Ps 28-29	Matt 12:38–45	
Oct-28	Ps 30-32	Ezek 42-43	Eph 6:21–24
	Ps 33	Matt 12:46–50	
Oct-29	Ps 34-35	Ezek 44-45	Phil 1:1–11
	Ps 36	Matt 13:1–23	
Oct-30	Ps 37-38	Ezek 46-47	Phil 1:12–26
	Ps 39	Matt 13:24–30	
Oct-31	Ps 40-42	Ezek 48	Phil 1:27–2:11
	Ps 43-44	Matt 13:31–35	
Nov-01	Ps 45-47	Dan 1-2	Phil 2:12–30
	Ps 48-49	Matt 13:36–52	
Nov-02	Ps 50-51	Dan 3	Phil 3:1–14
	Ps 52-54	Matt 13:53–14:12	
Nov-03	Ps 55-57	Dan 4-5	Phil 3:15–21
	Ps 58-59	Matt 14:13–21	
Nov-04	Ps 60-63	Dan 6	Phil 4:1–9
	Ps 64-65	Matt 14:22–36	
Nov-05	Ps 66-67	Dan 7-8	Phil 4:10–23
	Ps 68	Matt 15:1–20	
Nov-06	Ps 69-70	Dan 9-10	Col 1:1–14
	Ps 71	Matt 15:21–28	
Nov-07	Ps 72-73	Dan 11-12	Col 1:15–2:5
	Ps 74	Matt 15:29–39	
Nov-08	Ps 75-76	Hos 1-3	Col 2:6–15
	Ps 77	Matt 16:1–20	
Nov-09	Ps 78	Hos 4-7	Col 2:16–23
	Ps 79	Matt 16:21–28	
Nov-10	Ps 80-82	Hos 8-11	Col 3:1–17
	Ps 83	Matt 17:1–13	
Nov-11	Ps 84-86	Hos 12-14	Col 3:18–4:1
	Ps 87-88	Matt 17:14–27	

Calendar Of Scripture Readings

Nov-12	Ps 89	Joe 1-3	Col 4:2–18
	Ps 90	Matt 18:1–14	
Nov-13	Ps 91-93	Amo 1-4	1 Thess 1
	Ps 94-95	Matt 18:15–35	
Nov-14	Ps 96-98	Amo 5-9	1 Thess 2
	Ps 99-101	Matt 19:1–12	
Nov-15	Ps 102-103	Obad	1 Thess 3:1–5
	Ps 104	Matt 19:13–30	
Nov-16	Ps 105	Jon 1-4	1 Thess 3:6–4:12
	Ps 106	Matt 20:1–16	
Nov-17	Ps 107	Mic 1-7	1 Thess 4:13–18
	Ps 108	Matt 20:17–19	
Nov-18	Ps 109-110	Nah 1-3	1 Thess 5
	Ps 111-113	Matt 20:20–34	
Nov-19	Ps 114-116	Hab 1-3	2 Thess 1:1–2
	Ps 117-118	Matt 21:1–17	
Nov-20	Ps 119:1-40	Zeph 1-3	2 Thess 1:3–12
	Ps 119:41-88	Matt 21:18–27	
Nov-21	Ps 119:89-136	Hag 1-2	2 Thess 2
	Ps 119:137-176	Matt 21:28–46	
Nov-22	Ps 120-125	Zech 1-4	2 Thess 3:1–18
	Ps 126-129	Matt 22:1–14	
Nov-23	Ps 130-134	Zech 5-8	2 Pet 1:1–11
	Ps 135	Matt 22:15–22	
Nov-24	Ps 136-137	Zech 9-11	2 Pet 1:12–21
	Ps 138-139	Matt 22:23–40	
Nov-25	Ps 140-143	Zech 12-14	2 Pet 2
	Ps 144-145	Matt 22:41–23:12	
Nov-26	Ps 146-147	Mal 1-4	2 Pet 3
	Ps 148-150	Matt 23:13–39	

Abbreviations

Books of the Bible

1 Chr	First Chronicles	Hos	Hosea
1 Cor	First Corinthians	Is	Isaiah
1 John	First John	James	James
1 Kin	First Kings	Jer	Jeremiah
1 Pet	First Peter	Job	Job
1 Sam	First Samuel	Joel	Joel
1 Thess	First Thessalonians	John	John
1 Tim	First Timothy	Jon	Jonah
2 Chr	Second Chronicles	Josh	Joshua
2 Cor	Second Corinthians	Jude	Jude
2 John	Second John	Judg	Judges
2 Kin	Second Kings	Lam	Lamentations
2 Pet	Second Peter	Lev	Leviticus
2 Sam	Second Samuel	Luke	Luke
2 Thess	Second Thessalonians	Mal	Malachi
2 Tim	Second Timothy	Mark	Mark
3 John	Third John	Matt	Matthew
Acts	Acts	Mic	Micah
Amos	Amos	Nah	Nahum
Col	Colossians	Neh	Nehemiah
Dan	Daniel	Num	Numbers
Deut	Deuteronomy	Obad	Obadiah
Eccl	Ecclesiastes	Phil	Philippians
Eph	Ephesians	Philem	Philemon
Esth	Esther	Prov	Proverbs
Ex	Exodus	Ps	Psalms
Ezek	Ezekiel	Rev	Revelation
Ezra	Ezra	Rom	Romans
Gal	Galatians	Ruth	Ruth
Gen	Genesis	Song	Song of Solomon
Hab	Habakkuk	Titus	Titus
Hag	Haggai	Zech	Zechariah
Heb	Hebrew	Zeph	Zephaniah

Bibliography

Benedict, *St. Benedict's Rule for Monasteries*. Translated by Leonard J. Doyle. Project Gutenberg, May 16, 2021. www.gutenberg.org/cache/epub/50040/pg50040-images.html. Retrieved November 12, 2023.

Quigley, Edward J., *The Divine Office: A Study of the Roman Breviary*. Project Gutenberg, December 1, 2003. www.gutenberg.org/cache/epub/10058/pg10058.html. Retrieved November 1, 2023.

Huntington, William Reed. *A Short History of the Book of Common Prayer*. Project Gutenberg, January 5, 2021. www.gutenberg.org/cache/epub/30136/pg30136-images.html. Retrieved September 25, 2023.

Made in the USA
Columbia, SC
23 February 2024